110 Ways to Detect a Bad Relationship

If I can't be me, who can I be?

Be yourself – everyone else is taken

Oscar Wilde

Henriette Eiby Christensen

110 Ways to Detect a Bad Relationship
... Before it's too late

110 questions to ask yourself if you are in a
relationship or want to be

3rd Edition

Copyright © 2012 Henriette Eiby Christensen
www.henriettec.dk
www.110ways.com

Editor, English Version:
Vern Reo

Cover and Layout:
Henriette Eiby Christensen
Author portrait: Morten Pors www.mortenpors.dk
Web design: www.theroadthere.com

Published by HenrietteC
ISBN 978-87-995536-0-0

Henriette Eiby Christensen

I read Fay Weldon in the 1980's
I read Robin Norwood in the 1990's

I didn't get it.

I had to go through decades of misery before I got it.

I have simplified it for you.

Please get it!

Keep this book forever.

If you don't -
please donate it to a crisis center or a library

110 Ways to Detect a Bad Relationship

Henriette Eiby Christensen

From the Author:

The most recent research concludes that the brain isn't mature until we reach the ages between 25 and 30. This means that we can't 100% completely trust our brain, or perceive the consequences of our choices and actions until then. Is this why there are so many divorces? Waking up one day and all our choices are suddenly wrong? What now?

We get stuck. Stuck in an uncomfortable situation (if we are lucky).

Physical abuse is relatively easy to spot, as opposed to verbal abuse or bullying, which destroy people slowly and almost imperceptibly from within. Scars on the soul are invisible. Lots of people simply don't understand what happens to the other person if they bully.

I'm not a psychiatrist. I can't diagnose people, and I don't pretend I can. But I went from a bad relationship to worse, and I was driven to understand why so I wouldn't have to go through it again after divorce number two.

Nobody ever hit me. They left no tangible proofs of abuse. So why did I get stuck? Why wasn't I happy? *I didn't listen to my gut feeling*. I kept forgiving and I continued believing he would change. Of course he didn't. They rarely ever do unless they enter into long term therapy. Cognitive therapy is known to work, but

7

110 Ways to Detect a Bad Relationship

when I say long term, I mean a total commitment to weekly therapy for years. And when I say years, I mean a five year commitment. Think about this for a minute; what is five years compared to lifelong misery?

It took me 12 years to get out of a relationship and five more to figure out what happened. I hope to spare you all of that. And I hope to be able to make you aware of how you feel, and thus find the strength to not move in or to move on much sooner than I did because chances are – he won't change.

Almost anyone can become attracted to someone with a toxic personality. Almost anyone can get stuck in a bad relationship. Why? I'll try to answer that in this book.

How can you avoid it?

By noticing how you feel and appreciating your own self worth.
Does this sound like an ego trip? Well – read on.

For instance - a relationship with a psychopath or a sociopath is dangerous business. You lose touch with yourself and the world. You end up having no clue what is up or down – right or wrong, and then the stress will make you sick.

What are the common denominators for people with toxic personalities? It is someone who isn't nice to be around long term. Someone who keeps hurting you even though you make it clear what hurts, and who can put you under a spell so you stay despite your negative feelings and better judgment. Common sense evaporates.

You think you love him but you just aren't happy, and you have this gnawing feeling deep down – you just know it isn't good for you. You can have a million doubts, but having the courage to walk away from that is very empowering. He is not going to change, and if you try to make him change, you end up making things worse by hurting him and yourself.

If you have the tendency in finding people who make you miserable, you will have to remember this your whole life. Like an alcoholic who must always be aware of staying clear from that first drink ... for the rest of their life. Stay grounded in your own principles! **Never forget this!**

I will touch on the how's and why's, and encourage you to read more. Also, try joining the Facebook group and page: *110 Ways*.

Who am I to tell you what is right and wrong relationship wise? I am a single mother of three, twice divorced...

Please learn from my mistakes. Raising children by yourself is a lot of work.

**If a relationship isn't good –
why be in it?**

Henriette Eiby Christensen

Important Note

Before reading on, I need to emphasize the usage of the words "He", "Him", and "Boyfriend" are for simplicity sake. There are ample women who aren't nice to be around as well, so please interpret your situation accordingly.

Henriette Eiby Christensen

110 Ways to Detect a Bad Relationship

Never give more than you get.

Unknown

Thank You.

The tongue like a sharp knife ...
Kills without drawing blood.
Buddha

"Do you like him?"
"*I Love him*."
"Ahh, but do you *Like* him?"

Conversation with Robert Balter
Schenectady, NY ca. 1986

Henriette Eiby Christensen

If you are in a relationship you must assume 50% of the responsibility. If he hits or bullies you, you must leave – or assume 50% of the blame because you elected to stay.

If you find you are the bully, you will have to assume 90% of the healing process.
Think about that.

Learn from your mistakes.
Don't get bitten by the same dog twice coz
you're the victim just the 1st time.
After that, you're already a volunteer!

Jerose

Contents:

110 Ways to Detect a Bad Relationship

Henriette Eiby Christensen

Part 1

Courage doesn't always roar. Sometimes courage is the quiet voice at the end of the day saying, "I will try again tomorrow."

Mary Anne Radmacher

Your Notes

Henriette Eiby Christensen

How are you?

Why am I asking?

Does this have anything to do with relationships in general?

Yes it does, and I ask because *"how you are"* is your eternal, faithful guide, which is always there for you, and always knows the truth - Your Truth. Detecting a bad relationship (as strange as it may sound) can take a long time. It may even take years, but I will help you, and I hope this book finds you before you are stuck.

"The more of each other's needs you can fulfill the better the relationship."

Dr. Phillip McGraw

Ok – so tell me how...

All right – let me ask you something...

Does your boyfriend keep promises?

Yes? He's probably an ok guy

No? He might not be an ok guy

How difficult is that?

Does your boyfriend support you?

Yes? He's probably an ok guy

No? He might not be an ok guy

Henriette Eiby Christensen

Is he there for you if you are sick/tired/down/sad?

Yes

No

Is it ok with him if you want to go home early?

Yes

No

Henriette Eiby Christensen

Is it ok to go to separate events / parties?

Girl's night out?

Yes

No

Does he return borrowed things?

Yes

No

Does he have friends?

Yes

                But they are often ditched.

No

Do you like his friends?

Yes

No

Does he like his family?

Yes

No

110 Ways to Detect a Bad Relationship

Do you?

Yes

No

Does he like other people in general?

Yes

No

Do your friends and family like him?

Yes

No

Is he nice to kids?

Yes

No

110 Ways to Detect a Bad Relationship

Is he open?

Willing to share something that might be difficult?

Yes

No

Flexible?

Are changes of plans ok?

Yes

No

Is he honest?

Yes

No

Henriette Eiby Christensen

Does he respect confidentiality?

Can he keep a secret?

Yes

No

If he hurts your feelings – does he learn from it and refrains from repeating?

Yes

No

Are you at ease in his company?

Yes

No

Do you dare express your opinions?

Yes

No

Does he listen when you say no?

Yes

No

Do you feel safe when he is at the wheel?

Yes

No

Do you feel safe with him in general?

Yes

No

Is he considerate?

Yes

No

Is he able to compromise?

Yes

No

Are you?

110 Ways to Detect a Bad Relationship

Does he learn from mistakes?

Yes

No

Does he accept common sense?

Yes

No

Do you have many things in common?

> This will make it easier.

Yes

No

Can you trust him?

Yes

No

Is it okay to be giddy and perky?

Yes

No

Are spontaneity and changes of plans ok?

Yes

No

He says all the right things but does he follow through?

Yes

No

Does he keep appointments, come home when he said he would, or let you know if he is running late?

Yes

No

Do you always try to make sure he is comfortable? Does he for you as well?

Yes

No

Is he one of the good guys?

Yes

No

Would you consider having children with him?

Yes

No

Do you consider him to be a good role model?

Yes

No

Does he make you a better person?

Yes

No

Henriette Eiby Christensen

Ok – so you *love* him, or at least you think you do – but do you *like* him?

Yes

No

Can he be so very charming?

Alert!!!

Yes – be careful

No – be careful

**Charming can be a four-letter-word
Think about that.**

Henriette Eiby Christensen

Time to Turn...

110 Ways to Detect a Bad Relationship

Your Notes

Henriette Eiby Christensen

Part 2

Only when we are no longer afraid do we begin to live.

Dorothy Thompson

Your Notes

Henriette Eiby Christensen

Are you afraid of him?

Yes

No

Is he helpful, attentive, hospitable, generous, kind, funny – but mostly when others are present?

Yes

No

Is he governing, controlling, slick?

Yes

No

You ask him for a compliment, but he says being with him is enough of a compliment.

Yes

No

Does he think that "constructive criticism" equals praise?

Yes

No

Do you feel you have the need to defend yourself often?

Yes

No

Does he scold often?

Yes

No

Is he often irritable?

Yes

No

Is he overly sensitive to sounds?

Yes

No

110 Ways to Detect a Bad Relationship

Does he get restless easily?

Yes

No

Does he grab hold of you with hostile or threatening intent?

Yes

No

Beware:
 This can easily escalate into physical abuse.

He is mostly the one who gets his way?

Yes

No

Does he tell you exactly how things should be done but expects you to carry it out?

Yes

No

You agree on something but he does something else anyway. Probably without telling you?

Yes

No

He cancels on you often? At the last minute?

Yes

No

110 Ways to Detect a Bad Relationship

You ask him NOT to do something and he does it anyway?

Yes

Repeatedly?

No

Henriette Eiby Christensen

Does he get angry without any apparent reason?

Yes

No

Does he call you a *control freak* if you ask why he's late?

Yes

No

Does he think he is better than other people? Even family?

Yes

No

Does he think he is better than other people, but has no credentials? No recommendations?

Yes

> But he forged them.

No

Does he change jobs and friends often?

Yes

No

Does he keep you away from family and friends? Do they seem to slowly evaporate?

Yes

No

Can he put a wedge between you and your friends or family?

Yes

No

Does he bully?

You? Others?

Yes

No

Is he condescending? Sarcastic? Mean?

Yes

How does that feel?

No

Does he talk behind people's backs? His friends? Your friends? Family? You?

Yes

No

Is he very finicky? Or the opposite?

Yes

No

He can be very messy, but if you are, all hell breaks loose.

Yes

No

He likes doing things for other people, but rarely for you, and usually only for personal gain.

Yes

No

Are you the one who makes sure his children get up in the morning? That they are properly dressed? Do their homework? Have showers?

Yes

No

Does he boast?

Yes

No

Does he have childlike reactions?

As in disappointment, can't apologize, won't admit guilt, anger?

Yes

No

Henriette Eiby Christensen

Does he have a hard time being alone or living alone?

Yes

No

Does he use his job, sports, or games, drugs, alcohol as an escape?

Yes

No

Is he unwilling to help with chores?

Sits on the couch while you do everything?
Or asks you for help and when you help
he stops?

Yes

No

**Are you on edge in his presence –
afraid of how to act, or what to say?**

Yes

No

He has great empathy but only when it comes to fulfilling his own needs?

 Yes

No

Do you have to carefully consider your words around him?

Yes

No

Can he often talk you into something even when you're against it...
drawing you sometimes into a feeling of illness/nausea?

Yes

No

Does he put you down with words like: stupid, fat, ugly, wrinkled, old, disgusting, whore, nymphomaniac, witch, worthless, weakling, liar, bad person, incompetent, crazy etc.?

Yes

No

Does he ridicule or mock you – even in front of others?

Yes

No

110 Ways to Detect a Bad Relationship

Does he tell you it's your own fault?

Yes

No

Is he manipulative?

Yes

No

If you tell him something intimate about yourself, does he use it against you later?

Yes

No

Does he withhold conversation or sex as punishment?

Yes

No

He wants sex and refuses to take no for an answer.

Yes

No

He wants sex but refuses to protect you?

Condoms are such a nuisance.

Yes

How many has he been with?

No

Does he feel awkward about his body or performance?

Yes

No

Do you?

Does he threaten you with break up?

Yes

No

More than once?

Yes

No

Does he cheat on you?

Yes

No

Are you sure?

110 Ways to Detect a Bad Relationship

More than once?

Yes

No

Does your relationship have to be a secret?

Yes

No

Does he break things?

In anger? Perhaps only your things?

Yes

No

Henriette Eiby Christensen

Does he borrow things without asking?

Yes

No

Does he steal or throw your things out?

You suddenly can't find certain valuables or memorabilia

Yes

No

Henriette Eiby Christensen

Is he jealous?

Yes

No

Are you? Is there a tangible reason for that?

Does he check your cell phone, your mail, your diary? Your bank account?

Yes

No

Does he keep you on a short leash?

Yes

No

Does he have debts?

Yes, but it was unfortunate circumstances...

Was it really?

Yes

No

Maybe he has asked you to take up a loan?

In your name only?

Henriette Eiby Christensen

Is he honest to a fault?

What he says is hurtful.

Yes

No

Is it your fault when he gets angry, nasty mean or even physically abusive?

Yes

No

He apologizes and brings you flowers or gifts, but he does it again (and again)?

Yes

No

110 Ways to Detect a Bad Relationship

Can he make you apologize for something he did, or did to you?

Yes

No

Henriette Eiby Christensen

Can he make you feel like you did something wrong without you fully understanding why?

Yes

No

Do you find yourself making excuses for his bad behavior?

Yes

He is just really stressed, tired, had a bad day...

No

He apologizes for something he said or did but does it again anyway.

Yes

No

He apologizes, but the same argument keeps recurring?

Yes

No

Do you downplay what he does even if you feel ill about it?

Oh, it's not so bad...
He didn't mean to...
He didn't do it on purpose...
I walked into a door...

Yes

No

He says one thing but does something else?

Yes

No

Does he change his mind often?

Yes

No

Is he bossy?

Yes

No

Henriette Eiby Christensen

Does he have stubborn and/or raging opinions?

Yes

No

Is he judgmental? Racist?

Yes

No

Are you?

Henriette Eiby Christensen

Does he hate certain groups of people?

Yes

No

Can he make you feel insecure? Doubtful? Confused? Guilty? Humiliated?

Yes

No

Do you have to keep editing or second guessing yourself so you won't accidently push his buttons?

Yes

No

Walking on eggshells?

Are you in denial about the obvious?

Yes

No

Does he blame you for pushing his buttons?

Yes

No

Does he tease you to the point of tears?

Yes

No

Does he say you let him down?

Yes

No

No, I didn't start it. You're brokenhearted from a long long time ago...

Billy Joel

Does he drink? Too much in your opinion?

Yes

No

Drink and drive?

Yes

No

Does he lie?

Yes – but only to others...

Do you really believe that?

No

How difficult is that?

I'm not upset that you lied to me; I'm upset that from now on I can't believe you.
Friedrich Nietzsche

This is tricky. Everyone lies – it's not always a bad thing when placed into context.

Henriette Eiby Christensen

Does he punch the wall? You? Others? Himself?

Yes – how much? How often? Too much.

No

It is NEVER your fault if someone hits you.

Hitting is NEVER ok. Leave at once!

Hitting equals powerlessness.

Is he abusive to, or harm pets?

Yes

No

Cruelty to animals precedes cruelty to people

Do you have to protect others from him?

Yes

Is that ok?

No

Does he abuse drugs?

Yes

Is that ok?

No

Henriette Eiby Christensen

Does he call you a victim?

Yes

No

Does he steal?

Yes

No

**Does he downplay broken promises?
Criminal offences?**

Yes

No

Has he moved your boundaries for what is normal and ok?

Yes

No

Henriette Eiby Christensen

Do you talk behind people's backs now?

Do you run late now?

Do you stand people up now?

Do you drink more?

Do you smoke more?

Do drugs?

Need a sleeping pill?

Do you steal?

Do you feel you need to lie to protect yourself or others? Lie to yourself about how you really feel?

In other words: Has lying become a protection tool?...

How do you feel?

Good?

Happy?

Relaxed?

Do you sleep uneasily?

Stomach aches?

Headaches?

Erratic heart function?

Symptoms you've never had before?

Do you take pills now?

Do you feel sad?

Scared?

Nervous?

Depressed?

Are you afraid of him?

How many yes's and no's did you get?

What's my score?

I'm sorry – there is no fixed result – no way to tell exactly how many it takes to spot a bad relationship, because a single yes or no to the appropriate question may be enough to dissolve the relationship.

If you ask yourself "Should I stay or should I go." More than just once or twice, I would advise you to do the latter. It's not going to change.

How many yes's and no's can you live with?

What makes you feel good?

Everything I do I do it for you.

Bryan Adams

Is that the way it should be?

Or is that a potentially dangerous sentence?

110 Ways to Detect a Bad Relationship

Part one:

Yes is positive

Review your answers and check your gut
feeling – can you live with your answers?

Part two

Yes is negative

Review your answers and check your gut
feeling – can you live with your answers?

Your gut feeling NEVER lies.

Have the guts to listen!

How do you feel?

How are you really?

It's ok, you can tell me.

But can you admit to yourself that you aren't happy?

Henriette Eiby Christensen

Do you know if you like strawberries?

Or did you forget?

If you have forgotten, you will have to start by finding out what you *don't* like before you can figure out what you *do* like.

If you are headed in the wrong direction, God allows U-turns.

H. Jackson Brown Jr.

No one can make you feel inferior without your consent.

Eleanor Roosevelt

110 Ways to Detect a Bad Relationship

Again:

Would you like to stay with a person who isn't nice to be with in the long run? One who purposely keeps hurting you, even when you ask him not to? One who mesmerizes you to the point where you are likely to stay anyway?

I didn't think so...

Because:

No relationship is worth being miserable over.

Vern Reo

And:

If Love hurts it isn't Love.

don Miguel Ruiz

Your Notes

Henriette Eiby Christensen

Part 3

When you keep hoping and wishing he'll change.

Robin Norwood

Your Notes

Henriette Eiby Christensen

Consider this:

Why do I stay with him?

If he had an identical twin would I let my best friend, sister, or daughter date him?

What needs does he fulfill for me?

Might I be able to fulfill those needs myself or with friends?

Why can't I, or won't I let go, despite what my friends say?

110 Ways to Detect a Bad Relationship

Your Notes

Henriette Eiby Christensen

Part 4

Suffering makes you feel safe
because you know it so well

don Miguel Ruiz

Your Notes

Henriette Eiby Christensen

What?

Yes… what you are familiar with feels right. It may not feel good or nice or comfortable, but deep down in your subconscious, it feels right, it feels safe. If you grew up with a bunch of bullies for family members – that's what feels right. If you grew up with an alcoholic or abusive parent – that feels right. And the worst part is that it feels right despite the fact that you have promised yourself NEVER to live like that. You KNOW all the traps, and yet you find yourself in similar situations again and again, and they may even get worse and worse. Those are the patterns most difficult to break - the ones we grew up with. It takes everything we've got and more, and even then we might find ourselves in a situation like this: lightning strikes and we realize: *"Oh no, I'm just like my mom or dad)."* That hurts.

So, what can you do?

They all say "Stay true to yourself… Follow your heart… Listen to that little voice within… Trust your gut feeling." But what if you can't? What if you don't have those instincts? Well, don't worry. You will have to start by noticing what you like – like to do, to eat, to drink, to watch, to read… and then you'll have to start doing more of it, because the more you do things you like and appreciate, the more you'll value yourself, and the more you value yourself, the better you'll want to be treated AND treat other people. You see, this is not a selfish trip. We are interconnected. If you feel better, you'll have more to give. Be patient – it takes time.

But why? Why do we get stuck?

Well – one thing is having been encoded from home. Another is the ability some people have in making other people lose touch with themselves. How do they do that? They do it slowly – little by little by diminishing you – belittling you, and putting you down. You become insecure and easier to manipulate. Hypnotized in a sense. Most people can be hypnotized.

You forget who you are because there is always some truth to what they say, even if they are lying through their teeth.

Courage is the power to let go of the familiar.

Raymond Lindquist

Who can he/she be disguised as?

Anyone.

Moms, dads, siblings, lovers, friends, colleagues, the boss, your doctor, teacher, lawyer, the therapist, friends of friends, a random encounter...

Everyone can behave badly and inconsiderately from time to time. Everyone can mess up. But are they the same mistakes – the same hurtful behavior again and again? Just a few repetitive yes's or no's in the wrong places are actually plenty for us to be moving away from a sometimes balanced and good relationship.

There are many types of relationships, and you are the only one who can decide what's good for you. What will you accept? What do you feel good about? What do you think is realistic, and what do you feel you deserve?

Only you know your limits of when enough is enough!
It takes time. Begin by first allowing yourself to feel how you really do no matter how scary and painful that is. I can't stress it enough: *You will need help and support.*

Because you will have to go through the pain before you can get better.

Henriette Eiby Christensen

You can't spot a bad guy,
(he can be very handsome)
but you can feel how you are.

I didn't say it was easy...
Or maybe it is?

Is he considerate or inconsiderate?
Does he make you comfortable or uncomfortable?

50 Ways to Leave Your Lover

Paul Simon

Your Notes

Henriette Eiby Christensen

Who gets stuck in bad relationships?

People with great empathy.

Those who are susceptible to influence or persuasion.

People who take on excessive shares of responsibility, blame, and economy.

Those who practice benevolence, and want to please and help others.

People with damaged or low self-esteem.

Some of these are really positive and good which makes it so confusing when someone starts to use your best traits and abilities against you.

Never give anymore than you get!

Is that true?

Is it always true?

Henriette Eiby Christensen

The questions and answers in this book...

A toxic person can have many different diagnoses or problems. He can have a personality disorder as: psychopath, borderline, narcissist, or something else. Perhaps he's "just" an alcoholic, a manipulator or great egotist, or cannot be trusted or something else to different degrees. The point is that it does not feel good to be around them at length. It is hard to get away from them and almost impossible to explain, or for others to understand.

Maybe something just doesn't add up...

Your Notes

Henriette Eiby Christensen

Some Stress and Anxiety Symptoms.

You can develop Posttraumatic Stress Disorder **PTSD** from being bullied.

Headaches, migraines, tension, irregular heart rhythm, chest pain, difficulty breathing, dizziness, short-term memory issues, strange aches and pains, hives, fatigue, laziness, sensitivity to light and sound, increased tinnitus, irritability. Inability to experience pleasure, emotional, unusual sweating, the shakes, sleep deprivation, vision problems, nausea, anxiety, difficulty concentrating, loss of appetite, loss of sexual desire, depression, thoughts of suicide. PTSD. Disregard for: appearance, food, children, friends, hygiene, job, or aggressiveness – increased consumption of drugs, alcohol, sugar, food, and so on.

Get help ... see your doctor.

Your Notes

Preventive Measures:

Listen to your gut feeling and trust it. When in doubt – let the relationship go. Trust your decision to be the right one for you in the long run. Don't look back.

Stay true to who you are and what you want. If you don't know what that is, start by finding out what you like – and don't like.

It is ok to be a homemaker, but it is important to have something to fall back on, like an education or special skills.

Keep your independence.

Keep your own friends, family, and network.

Ask your friends, family, and his friends about your new boyfriend and listen to what they say.

What kind of friends does he have? Nice ones?

And what about his family? Do you like them?

Get to know yourself.

Take yourself out on a date and ask the questions you'd ask another person in order to get to know them.

You allowing yourself to be you, sets you free.

Panache Desai

Healthy Relationships

ACCOUNTABILITY
- Accepting responsibility, behaviors, and attitudes
- Admitting mistakes (or being wrong)

SAFETY
- Refusing to intimidate or manipulate
- Respecting physical space
- Expressing self nonviolently and honestly

TRUST
- Accepting each other's word
- Giving the benefit of the doubt

RESPECT

HONESTY
- Communication openly and truthfully

COOPERATION
- Asking, not expecting
- Accepting change
- Making decisions together
- Being willing to compromise
- Seeking mutually satisfying resolutions to conflict

SUPPORT
- Supporting each other's choices
- Being understanding
- Offering encouragement
- Listening non-judgementally
- Valuing opinions

http://safe.unc.edu/files/2011/06/healthy-relationships1.gif

Henriette Eiby Christensen

Give him no more than three chances. Remember that:

No more than three!

And if he hits you?
GET OUT NOW! No more chances.

There is no excuse for hitting.
Get out before it's too late.

I'm the most honest person in the world.
....NOOO! You are the most un-empathic, tactless person in the world, and you use "honesty" as abuse.

Henriette Eiby Christensen

Tools from *THEO:*

"Is there something I have done to you that makes
you treat me this way?"
"Yes" *– discuss it.*
"My feelings were very hurt when..."
*"****No****" – war is over. Leave.*

Anger is usually an expression of hurt.

"You are not allowed to treat me in this manner."

**When you are uncomfortable enough you will
change.**
Hold your boundaries!
Recognize what you don't want.
Ask for help from your friends and community.

110 Ways to Detect a Bad Relationship

Your Notes

Henriette Eiby Christensen

But what about forgiveness?

I know – we were all taught to forgive and keep forgiving – to turn the other cheek.

If forgiving means that you have to keep being miserable, it doesn't make sense. Forgiving is a tool to help you let go of negative emotions and thoughts. Negative emotions drain you, and steal your life and happiness. If you forgive, you don't have to think about it anymore. You are free. You are also free to move on because exposing yourself to abuse of any kind, is not ok. *"Love thy neighbor as thy self"*. What I'm saying is; **forgive the other person for your own sake.** Love yourself first. Forgive yourself. When you love and forgive yourself, you can love and forgive others.

He might ask you for forgiveness. He might ask you for patience and understanding. He may tell you about his miserable childhood so you'll feel sorry for him and stay, or something to that effect. I mean you can't leave someone who is down, can you? Should you? He might tell you he will change. These are traps if they happen more than once. If you don't fall prey to them and you put your foot down he might learn – if you don't – he never will and he'll keep hurting you. Standing up for yourself and standing firm can be very scary. Do it anyway. It's very rewarding and you will be happy you did. In fact, you will never regret it, and you will grow stronger and stronger for each time. Also, remember that you can't fix him. Accept him or not. Does he have a need to change who and what you are? Have a serious talk together,and seek out the necessary answers if you are good for one another.

If you agree on most things, life together will be a lot easier.

Not forgiving someone is like drinking poison and expecting the other person to die.
Unknown

Choose carefully who you have children with.

Toxicity may not show up for years – it can be triggered by a crisis like the death of a close friend or relative, having a baby, getting fired, failing an exam etc.
You will have to stay aware and awake for the rest of your life. Stay grounded. Keep listening to your gut.

Henriette Eiby Christensen

Questions to be considered:

Which one affects the victim the most: Physical or verbal abuse? Why?

Why is *charming* being compared to a four-letter-word?

Among other things you can become addicted to drugs and alcohol. Can you become addicted to a person? How and why?

What is codependency?

Why is lying tricky?

Of all the questions, which ones hit home the most?

For yourself, or for someone you know? Someone close?

Why are there so many closely related questions?

Why don't people leave abusive relationships?

Consider the statement: "It's only verbal."

Why is it important to know what you like?

Look up PTSD.

Your Notes

Henriette Eiby Christensen

Misery Loves Company

Feeling miserable is not just a bad habit. I firmly believe it can be compared to being addicted, and you can use Robin Norwood's ten point recovery plan from the book: "Women Who Love too Much". Simplified here:

1. Get help

2. Make your recovery the most important thing in your life

3. Locate a support group

4. Develop your spiritual side through daily exercises

5. Stop controlling others

6. Learn how to stop getting involved in mind games

7. Courageously face your problems and shortcomings

8. Cultivate the weaker sides of yourself

9. Develop: "Sacred Selfishness"

10. Share your experience with others and help them

And I'd like to add:

11. Stay aware and awake for the rest of your life.

110 questions?

One question is really enough.

How are you really?

POWER AND CONTROL

PHYSICAL **VIOLENCE** SEXUAL

USING COERCION AND THREATS
Making and/or carrying out threats to do something to hurt her • threatening to leave her, to commit suicide, to report her to welfare • making her drop charges • making her do illegal things.

USING INTIMIDATION
Making her afraid by using looks, actions, gestures • smashing things • destroying her property • abusing pets • displaying weapons.

USING ECONOMIC ABUSE
Preventing her from getting or keeping a job • making her ask for money • giving her an allowance • taking her money • not letting her know about or have access to family income.

USING EMOTIONAL ABUSE
Putting her down • making her feel bad about herself • calling her names • making her think she's crazy • playing mind games • humiliating her • making her feel guilty.

USING MALE PRIVILEGE
Treating her like a servant • making all the big decisions • acting like the "master of the castle" • being the one to define men's and women's roles

USING ISOLATION
Controlling what she does, who she sees and talks to, what she reads, where she goes • limiting her outside involvement • using jealousy to justify actions.

USING CHILDREN
Making her feel guilty about the children • using the children to relay messages • using visitation to harass her • threatening to take the children away.

MINIMIZING, DENYING AND BLAMING
Making light of the abuse and not taking her concerns about it seriously • saying the abuse didn't happen • shifting responsibility for abusive behavior • saying she caused it.

PHYSICAL **VIOLENCE** SEXUAL

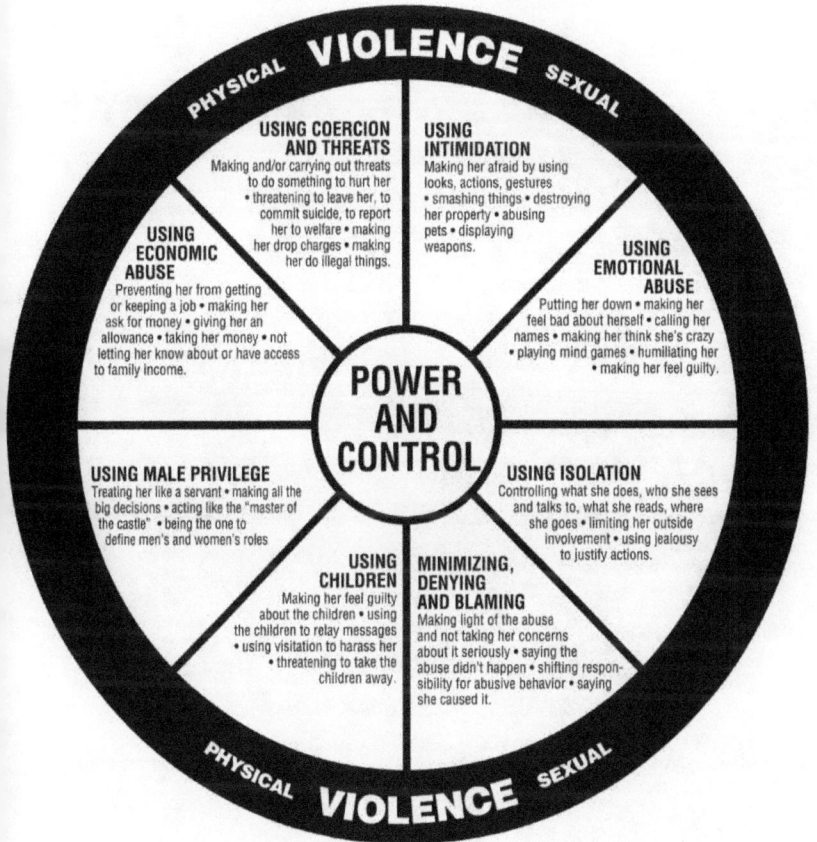

DOMESTIC ABUSE INTERVENTION PROJECT
202 East Superior Street
Duluth, MN 55802
218-722-2781
www.theduluthmodel.org

110 Ways to Detect a Bad Relationship

What War on Women?

3,073
killed in terror
attacks in the US

2,002
US troops killed
in Afghanistan

4,486
US troops killed
in Iraq

11,766
American
women killed
by their
husbands or
boyfriends:
more than the
above
categories
combined.

Figures from 9/10/2001 to 6/6/2012. Each dot equals one death. Domestic violence stats via Federal Bureau of Investigation. If a loved one is hurting you call 1 (800) 799-SAFE.

Henriette Eiby Christensen

Can one be unknowingly bullying?

Let me start out with an extreme example.

I have written five books on bullying in relationships in Danish.

A man read my first book and wrote me that he was in shock. He had no idea how the way he had been treating/talking to his wife (who had killed herself years earlier) and various girlfriends might have affected them.

Obviously it made him think deep. He thought he had been a good husband and father – no cheating, no excessive drinking, no drugs, no stealing... but...

I find that people don't even know they might be condescending or putting others down. Being bossy, judgmental and sarcastic seem to be generally acceptable.

It is in the way that you say things – it can be very subtle, but also very damaging in the long run. How you may say something like "Well, your sister would never do something like that...", "My ex girlfriend always...". You may say you'll do something, but you "forget".

So why can't we spot such behavior by ourselves? It is really quite simple. We were brought up that way. That's how our parents and friends talked to us, and to their partners or friends. It has become normal and second nature, and we have forgotten the initial hurt.

You may say we have become callused, and we unwittingly pass it on to the next generation.

Try watching yourself over the coming weeks. Watch how people react when you speak to them, especially if you are upset with them. Look into their eyes. Is your spouse or child candid, or do they fidget when you talk to them? Do they look scared?

It's all about awareness.

Henriette Eiby Christensen

What if I can't leave?

It often takes a long time to leave a charming person you have feelings for. If you find yourself asking the "should I stay or should I go" question more than once... You should try writing down the times and episodes where he has hurt you or let you down. I'm not telling you to carry a grudge, but to gain clarity of mind because we tend to forget and forgive way too often.

Remember:

No more than three chances.

If you are in a relationship where you find the need to belittle yourself, and where you are trying not to shine too brightly or he will get mad/jealous/condescending ... that might be even worse than others belittling you because you are undermining yourself, and you will lose touch with who, and what you are really meant to be.

Your Notes

Henriette Eiby Christensen

NOW WHAT????

Ok now you can feel what you feel…

You are confused and hurt.

How do you move on?

You'll need to stay in the feeling of hurt for a while and remember everything.

Why? It's so uncomfortable.

I know – I've been there. But, if you don't stay there long enough to feel really sick about it, you are much more likely to go back to a bad relationship, or find another one like it only slightly different so you don't recognize it right away. Chances are – you will find yourself stuck again.

Hang on to this book as a life raft.

Start being good to yourself, each and every day. It can be a small thing like eating an apple really slowly – relishing every bite. Try picking a flower for yourself, reading a magazine, or taking a walk. Whatever makes you feel better.

Read Positive Psychology. Keep at it. ***Every single day!***

Writing everything down and reviewing those words from time to time has a wonderful therapeutic effect, which will help you heal and not make the same mistakes again and again.

Never chase love, affection, or attention. If it isn't given freely by another person it isn't worth having.

Unknown

Your Notes

Henriette Eiby Christensen

Summary:

Here are five of the biggest telltale signs you are in a verbally abusive relationship plus five ways you can start helping yourself:

In no particular order:

1. You are nervous around him. (Walking on eggshells.)
2. His needs come first. (You drop everything at his call.)
3. Your friends and family disappear. (They aren't good enough for you – he says.)
4. You suffer from various stress and anxiety symptoms. (Stomach and headaches, insomnia, dizziness, depression etc.)
5. You complain to yourself or other people about him.

a. Take a minute to breathe and do nothing.
b. Do something nice for yourself every day – even if it is just picking a flower, gazing out the window for a few extra minutes or eating an apple really slowly savoring the taste, smell and the beauty.
   Plan it a day ahead so you have something to look forward to.
c. Call a long lost friend or family member and go out for coffee or a walk.
d. Talk to a therapist or your family doctor – if that is out of the question – Google PTSD and read about it. You can develop PTSD from being bullied – it doesn't have to take a war.

And the toughest one:

Listen to yourself. Really listen. Are you willing to live
like this for the rest of your life?

Why is this, the toughest one?
Because you will have to face yourself – honestly –
maybe for the first time ever.
When I did this I almost became suicidal – if that
happens you'll know that you'll need to change
something and you will need help.

Find people who understand.

Henriette Eiby Christensen

Where to get help:

Worldwide
www.hotpeachpages.net

USA
National Domestic Violence Hotline
1-800-799-SAFE (800-799-7233)
www.thehotline.org

Alcoholics Anonymous
www.aa.org

Drug Addicts Anonymous
daausa.org

Suicide Hotlines
suicidehotlines.com

Center Against Domestic Violence
www.cadvny.org

Help for Abused & Battered Women
Domestic Violence Shelters
www.helpguide.org

Abuse Victim Hotline
www.avhotline.org

RAINN – Rape, Abuse and Incest National Network
www.rainn.org

UK
www.adviceguide.org.uk/england/domestic_violence

France
Fédération Nationale Solidarité Femmes - FNSF
www.solidaritefemmes.org

Your school counselor
Your church
Facebook groups

www.110ways.com

Henriette Eiby Christensen

Where to get help in Denmark:

www.depnet.dk

www.anonyme-alkoholikere.dk

www.anti-stalking.dk

www.lokk.dk

www.mandecentret.dk

www.mandens.dk

www.moedrehjaelpen.dk

www.dannerhuset.dk

www.voldmodkvinder.dk

www.udenhensyn.dk

www.facebook.com:
Trolde om mennesker som har andre i deres vold

Please go get help!

Life is short and you deserve to be happy. Please honor yourself.

Please learn from my mistakes.

Life is too short for spending time with people, who complicate your life.

Hans Henrik Nielsen

Henriette Eiby Christensen

Definitions of a psychopath:

http://en.wikipedia.org/wiki/Psychopathy

http://psychcentral.com/news/2006/07/03/improving-the-definheion-of-%E2%80%98psychopath%E2%80%99/64.html

To learn more and find help Google these in your own language: psychopath, narcissist, borderline, sociopath, bipolar, toxic personalities, personality disorders, character disturbance, stress or anxiety symptoms.
Domestic/Verbal/Emotional/Psychological Abuse
Safe House, Crisis Center etc.

Take your life in your own hands and what happens?

A terrible thing:

> ***No one to blame.***

Erica Jong

Henriette Eiby Christensen

Make a drawing
of yourself. What
do you look like
in five years?
Are you happy?

If you are not happy, what have you got to give?

110 Ways to Detect a Bad Relationship

You are *not* alone.

Henriette Eiby Christensen

Recommended:

"Women who Love too much" by Robin Norwood

"Snakes in Suits" by Paul Babiak and Robert D. Hare

"The Missing Piece Meets the Big O" by Shel Silverstein

"Relationship Rescue" by Phillip McGraw

"Character Disturbance—The Phenomenon of Our Age"
by George K. Simon, Ph.D

"Manual of the Core Value Workshop"
by Steven Stosny, Ph.D.

"The *Powerful* Self: A Workbook of Therapeutic Self-Empowerment" by Steven Stosny, Ph.D.

A free, one hour movie about a self-proclaimed psychopath:
http://topdocumentaryfilms.com/i-psychopath/

A sister Book:

110 Ways to Charm Your Brain

Positive Thinking

Honor your heart's desire

Jewels collected since The Secret.

Hundreds of exercises and questions to keep you on track on your road to happiness.

Courage is the power to let go of the familiar.

Raymond Lindquist

Henriette Eiby Christensen

110 Ways – the series:

110 Ways to Detect a Bad Relationship –
Before it's Too Late

110 Ways to Charm Your Brain –
Positive Thinking

110 Ways to Avoid Getting Old –
Sparkle Your Life

110 Ways to Spot a Toxic Person –
I Love No-One

110 Ways – First Book of Quotes –
Happiness

In the works:
110 Ways to Build a Good Relationship –
Yes! Another Day with You!

110 Ways – Second Book of Quotes –
Abundance

Co-author of:
The Faces Behind the Pages that Inspire
Published by A Victim No More

229

Find the group and page on Facebook:
www.facebook.com/110Ways

www.110ways.com
www.facebook.com/110Ways

Henriette Eiby Christensen

www.ingramcontent.com/pod-product-compliance
Lightning Source LLC
Chambersburg PA
CBHW021051090426
42738CB00006B/285